Big Machines

LOADERS

By Katie Kawa

Gareth Stevens
Publishing

Please visit our website, www.garethstevens.com. For a free color catalog of all our high-quality books, call toll free 1-800-542-2595 or fax 1-877-542-2596.

Library of Congress Cataloging-in-Publication Data

Kawa, Katie.
Loaders / Katie Kawa.
     p. cm. — (Big machines)
Includes index.
ISBN 978-1-4339-5568-6 (pbk.)
ISBN 978-1-4339-5569-3 (6-pack)
ISBN 978-1-4339-5566-2 (library binding)
1. Loaders (Machines)—Juvenile literature. I. Title.
TL296.5.K38 2012
621.8'6—dc22

                                               2011006514

First Edition

Published in 2012 by
Gareth Stevens Publishing
111 East 14th Street, Suite 349
New York, NY 10003

Copyright © 2012 Gareth Stevens Publishing

Editor: Katie Kawa
Designer: Daniel Hosek

Photo credits: Cover, pp. 1, 5, 7, 9, 11, 17, 19, 21, 23, 24 (all) Shutterstock.com; pp. 13, 15 Thinkstock.com.

Printed in the United States of America

CPSIA compliance information: Batch #CS11GS: For further information contact Gareth Stevens, New York, New York at 1-800-542-2595.

Contents

How Loaders Work 4

Wheel Loaders. 16

On the Job 20

Words to Know 24

Index. 24

A loader is a kind
of tractor.

A loader has two arms.

7

A loader has a bucket.
The bucket carries things.

Loaders carry dirt and rocks.

Loaders work with dump trucks. They put things in the trucks.

13

Some loaders dig! They dig up dirt before they move it.

One kind of loader is a wheel loader. It has four wheels.

17

Wheel loaders are used in the city. They can go on roads.

19

A loader uses a plow.
The plow moves snow.

Loaders carry bricks for new houses.

23

Words to Know

bricks

bucket

Index

bucket 8
plow 20

tractor 4
wheel loader
16, 18

24